# Shadows and Spectrum

## Unraveling the Psychology of Gender and Sexuality

**Freudian Trips**

# Copyright Page

© 2023 by Freudian Trips

All rights reserved. No part of this book may be reproduced in any form or by any electronic or mechanical means, including information storage and retrieval systems, without permission in writing from the publisher, except by a reviewer who may quote brief passages in a review.

This book is a work of non-fiction. Unless otherwise noted, the author and the publisher make no explicit guarantees as to the accuracy of the information contained in this book and will not be held responsible for any errors or omissions.

Published by Omniterra Media Inc

First Edition

Visit the author's website at www.freudiantrips.com

# Disclaimer

# Chapter 1: Introduction: Setting the Scene

## Overview of Gender and Sexuality Psychology

Welcome to the fascinating world of gender and sexuality psychology! This field of study delves into how we understand and express our gender and sexuality, two integral aspects of our identity. The roles, actions, characteristics, and behaviors that a society views as proper for men, women, and non-binary people—those who don't exactly identify as male or female—are referred to as gender. Sexuality, on the other hand, is about how we experience and express ourselves as sexual beings, which includes whom we're attracted to, our sexual preferences, and how we perceive our sexual identity.

The study of gender and sexuality psychology isn't just about understanding definitions. It's about exploring the deep and often complex ways these aspects of our identity impact our lives, relationships, and even our mental health. It's about understanding ourselves and others in a more profound and empathetic way.

## The Evolving Landscape of Gender and Sexual Identity

Gender and sexuality are far from being static concepts; they are dynamic and ever-evolving. Historically, many cultures recognized only two genders (male and female) and considered heterosexual relationships as the norm. However, this perspective has been changing dramatically. Today, we acknowledge a spectrum of gender identities, like transgender, genderqueer, and agender, among others. Similarly, sexual orientation is now understood to be more than just heterosexual or homosexual; it includes bisexual, pansexual, asexual, and many more identifications.

This evolution is not just a change in terminology; it's a shift in understanding human diversity and complexity. It's about recognizing and respecting each person's unique experience and expression of their gender and sexuality. This changing landscape is crucial for fostering a more inclusive and accepting society.

**Objectives and Scope of the Book**

This book aims to be your guide through the intricate and colorful world of gender and sexuality psychology. We'll embark on a journey to explore various aspects of this field:

We'll start by looking at the historical context of gender and sexuality, understanding how our current perspectives were shaped.

We'll delve into the biological, psychological, and social factors that influence gender and sexual identity.

We'll explore how gender and sexuality intersect with other aspects of identity like race, culture, and socioeconomic status.

We'll discuss the challenges faced by individuals who diverge from societal norms and how they navigate these challenges.

Finally, we'll look towards the future, contemplating emerging trends and how they might shape our understanding of gender and sexuality.

Throughout this journey, we aim to make this book accessible and engaging for everyone, regardless of your prior knowledge of the subject. We'll avoid complex jargon and explain concepts in simple, everyday language. By the end of this book, we hope you'll have a deeper understanding and appreciation of the diversity and richness of human gender and sexual identity.

So, let's set sail on this enlightening journey to understand the vibrant tapestry of human gender and sexuality!

# Chapter 2: Historical Perspectives

## Early Theories of Gender and Sexuality

Long ago, understanding gender and sexuality was quite different from today's perspectives. In early societies, gender roles were strictly defined: men were often hunters and protectors, while women were gatherers and caretakers. These roles were thought to be natural and unchangeable. Sexuality, too, was seen through a limited lens, primarily focused on reproduction.

As time went on, philosophers and thinkers began to question and explore these ideas. For instance, in ancient Greece, there was an acknowledgment of same-sex relationships, but these were often seen through the prism of social status rather than a genuine understanding of sexual orientation.

Fast forward to the 19th and early 20th centuries, when psychologists like Sigmund Freud began to explore sexuality and gender more deeply. Freud introduced the idea that sexuality was a fundamental human drive and developed theories about how childhood experiences shape adult gender and sexual identities. However, his theories, now considered outdated, often linked homosexuality to developmental issues, reflecting the biases of that era.

## The Influence of Culture and Society Through Ages

Culture and society have always played a massive role in shaping ideas about gender and sexuality. For example, during the Victorian era, there was a strict moral code regarding sexual behavior, especially for women. This era saw the rise of the notion that women were naturally less sexual than men, a stereotype that persisted for a long time.

In different cultures, there have been various understandings of gender and sexuality. Some Native American tribes recognized two-spirit people, who combined male and female traits in ways that were unique and respected. Similarly, in parts of South Asia, hijras (transgender individuals) have been acknowledged, though often marginalized, for centuries.

## Milestones in Gender and Sexuality Psychology

The 20th century brought significant shifts. The feminist movement challenged traditional gender roles, advocating for women's rights and equality. This movement brought greater awareness to the fact that gender roles were socially constructed, not biologically determined.

The 1950s and 1960s saw a revolution in how sexuality was viewed, partly thanks to researchers like Alfred Kinsey. Kinsey's studies revealed that human sexual behavior was far more diverse than previously thought, challenging many societal norms.

In the late 20th and early 21st centuries, the understanding of gender expanded further. The transgender rights movement gained momentum, advocating for recognition and rights for people whose gender identity does not align with the sex they were assigned at birth.

These milestones mark a journey from rigid, prescribed roles to a more fluid and inclusive understanding of gender and sexuality. Today, psychology recognizes that both are complex, influenced by a combination of biological, psychological, and social factors.

In summary, the history of gender and sexuality psychology is a story of evolving understanding and acceptance. From rigid, traditional roles to a recognition of the rich diversity of human experience, this journey reflects a growing respect for the individual's right to define their own identity. As we look back on this history, we gain a clearer picture of the challenges and triumphs that have shaped our current understanding of gender and sexuality.

# Chapter 3: Biological Underpinnings

## The Role of Genetics and Hormones

Let's start with genetics and hormones, two key players in our biological makeup. Genetics is like a blueprint for your body, containing instructions on everything from your eye color to, to some extent, your gender and sexual traits. But it's not a strict set of plans. Think of it more like guidelines that can be interpreted in various ways.

Hormones, on the other hand, are the body's chemical messengers. They play a big role in developing sexual and reproductive organs and in determining characteristics like muscle mass and voice pitch. Hormones like testosterone and estrogen are often associated with male and female traits, respectively, but the truth is more complex. Everyone has a mix of these hormones, and their levels can vary widely among individuals.

It's important to understand that while genetics and hormones influence gender and sexuality, they don't dictate them. Human behavior and identity are the results of a complex interplay between biology, environment, and personal experiences.

## Brain Structure and Function in Gender and Sexuality

Now, let's talk about the brain, our body's command center. Studies show some differences in brain structures and activity patterns between men and women. But these differences are subtle and variable. They don't translate into hard and fast rules about gender behavior or identity.

For example, you might have heard that men are naturally better at math while women are better at language skills. In reality, these differences are minor and greatly influenced by social expectations and upbringing.

When it comes to sexuality, things get even more complex. There's no definitive "gay brain" or "straight brain." Sexual orientation appears to result from a mix of genetic, hormonal, and environmental influences, and it's not something determined by any one part of the brain.

## Debunking Biological Determinism Myths

Biological determinism is the idea that biology is destiny, that our genes and biology strictly determine things like behavior, intelligence, and sexual orientation. But this is a myth. Why? Because it ignores the significant roles of environment, culture, and personal choice.

For example, the idea that men are naturally aggressive and women are naturally nurturing is a stereotype that doesn't hold up under scrutiny. Such traits are heavily influenced by how we're raised and the cultural norms we're exposed to.

In the realm of sexuality, the myth that people are "born this way" oversimplifies a complex reality. While biology plays a role, it's not the whole story. People's understanding and expression of their sexuality can change over time, influenced by a myriad of factors beyond their genes.

In conclusion, this chapter shows that while biology is an important piece of the puzzle in understanding gender and sexuality, it's not the whole picture. Our identities and behaviors are shaped by a dynamic mix of biology, environment, and personal experiences, making each of us unique in our own way. Understanding this helps us appreciate the rich diversity of human gender and sexuality, beyond just the biological lens.

# Chapter 4: Sexual Orientation and Behavior

## Defining Sexual Orientation: A Complex Tapestry

Sexual orientation is about who you are attracted to emotionally, romantically, and sexually. It's like having a built-in compass that guides who you find appealing. This compass can point towards people of the opposite gender, the same gender, both genders, or even no gender at all. Heterosexual refers to attraction to the opposite gender, homosexual refers to attraction to the same gender, bisexual refers to attraction to both genders, and asexual refers to little to no sexual attraction to any gender.

But here's the key: sexual orientation is more like a spectrum than a set of neat categories. Imagine a rainbow. Just as there are many shades between the distinct colors of a rainbow, there's a wide range of attractions and experiences in human sexuality. Some people may find their orientation doesn't change much over their lifetime, while for others, it may be more fluid and changeable.

## Behavioral Aspects of Sexuality

How we express our sexual orientation in our behavior can vary greatly. For instance, two people might both identify as homosexual but have very different ways of expressing their sexuality. One might be open and public about their relationships, while the other might be more private.

It's important to remember that sexual behavior and sexual orientation aren't always perfectly aligned. There are many reasons, including cultural and social factors, why someone might behave in ways that don't seem to match their orientation.

## Societal Attitudes and Their Psychological Impacts

Society's attitudes towards different sexual orientations have varied greatly over time and across cultures. Unfortunately, not all of these attitudes have been accepting. Discrimination and stigma against non-heterosexual orientations have caused significant psychological stress and harm. This can lead to feelings of isolation, depression, and even to mental health crises.

Thankfully, there's been a positive shift in many parts of the world towards greater acceptance and understanding of diverse sexual orientations. This change has been hugely beneficial. Studies have shown that accepting environments significantly improve the mental health and well-being of individuals with diverse sexual orientations.

In conclusion, understanding sexual orientation as a complex, varied, and deeply personal aspect of human experience is key. It's not just about who we're attracted to, but also about how we navigate our identities in a world that's still learning to embrace diversity. Recognizing the spectrum of human sexuality and the importance of a supportive, accepting society is crucial for the psychological health and happiness of everyone.

# Chapter 5: Psychological Theories and Models

In this chapter, we'll dive into some of the key theories and models psychologists use to understand gender and sexuality. Don't worry, we'll keep it simple and relatable!

**Psychoanalytic Perspectives on Gender and Sexuality**

First up is the psychoanalytic perspective, which originated with Sigmund Freud. Freud was like a detective of the mind, exploring how our unconscious thoughts and early childhood experiences shape our personalities, including our gender and sexual identities. He suggested that our early relationships, particularly with parents, play a big role in how we see ourselves and others in terms of gender and sexuality.

However, it's important to note that many of Freud's ideas, like the Oedipus complex (where a child feels a deep attraction to the opposite-sex parent), are considered outdated and overly simplistic today. Modern psychology recognizes that gender and sexuality are much more complex and influenced by a broader range of factors.

## Cognitive-Behavioral Approaches

Next, let's talk about cognitive-behavioral approaches. This is like looking at the software of the mind. It's about understanding how our thoughts (cognitions) and actions (behaviors) interact with each other. For example, if a person believes that being attracted to the same gender is wrong (a cognition), they might feel anxious or depressed (emotional response) and avoid relationships (behavior).

Cognitive-behavioral therapy (CBT) is often used to help people challenge and change unhelpful thoughts and beliefs about gender and sexuality, leading to healthier behaviors and emotional well-being.

## Queer Theory and Postmodern Perspectives

Lastly, we have queer theory and postmodern perspectives. These approaches are like the rebels of psychology, challenging traditional ideas and norms. Queer theory questions categories like 'male' and 'female' or 'gay' and 'straight', arguing that these categories are too limiting and don't capture the full diversity of human experience. It sees gender and sexuality as fluid and socially constructed, meaning they're shaped by cultural and societal norms rather than being fixed biological traits.

Postmodern perspectives, on the other hand, emphasize the role of language, power dynamics, and social constructs in shaping our understanding of gender and sexuality. They encourage us to look at how society's narratives and discourses (like media, laws, and education) impact our views and experiences of gender and sexuality.

In summary, psychological theories and models offer different lenses through which we can understand gender and sexuality. From the deep dives into our unconscious minds with psychoanalysis, to the practical, thought-focused approaches of CBT, to the challenging and boundary-pushing views of queer and postmodern theories, each provides unique insights into the complex tapestry of human identity. Understanding these theories helps us appreciate the many factors that shape who we are and how we express ourselves.

# Chapter 6: Intersectionality in Gender and Sexuality

**The Intersection of Gender, Sexuality, Race, and Class**

Imagine gender and sexuality as two colors on a canvas. Now add race and class, each a different color. When these colors blend, they create unique shades and patterns. This is the essence of intersectionality. It's about how different aspects of our identity – like gender, sexuality, race, and class – intersect and shape our experiences.

For example, a black woman's experience of gender is influenced by her race, and a gay man's experience of sexuality is influenced by his social class. Each combination of identities brings its own set of challenges and experiences. A wealthy, white gay man may face less discrimination than a poor, black transgender woman. Understanding these intersections helps us see the full picture of someone's life.

**Impacts of Intersectionality on Mental Health**

These intersections don't just affect our social experiences; they also impact our mental health. Facing discrimination for one aspect of your identity is hard enough, but dealing with multiple layers of discrimination can be overwhelming. For instance, someone who is both gay and from a racial minority might experience homophobia as well as racism, adding layers of stress and emotional strain.

This kind of chronic stress can lead to higher rates of mental health issues like anxiety and depression. It's important to understand that these mental health challenges are often a response to external pressures and prejudices, not something inherently wrong with the individual.

## Empirical Studies and Personal Experiences

Research and real-life stories back up these ideas. Studies have shown that people who belong to multiple marginalized groups often face higher levels of discrimination and have less access to resources like healthcare and social support. This lack of support and increased discrimination can make it harder to cope with mental health issues.

Personal experiences also highlight the importance of intersectionality. Listening to the stories of people who navigate these complex identities can teach us a lot. It's not just about statistics; it's about real people's lives and struggles. These stories can inspire us to work towards a more inclusive and understanding society.

In conclusion, understanding the intersectionality in gender and sexuality is crucial for a comprehensive understanding of human experience. It's about recognizing that each person's identity is a unique blend of various factors, and these combinations can significantly impact their life and mental health. By acknowledging and respecting these intersections, we can better support and advocate for everyone's well-being and rights.

# Chapter 7: The Role of Society and Culture

**Social Constructs of Gender and Sexuality**

Think of society and culture as a big stage where the roles of gender and sexuality are often scripted by traditions, norms, and expectations. These roles are social constructs, which means they are ideas created and accepted by societies rather than being unchangeable biological facts. For instance, the belief that pink is for girls and blue is for boys is a social construct, not a natural law.

In different cultures, these constructs vary greatly. What is considered masculine or feminine in one culture might be viewed differently in another. These constructs are not just about clothing or colors; they extend to how we are expected to behave, feel, and interact with others based on our gender and sexuality.

**Media Influence and Representation**

Media is like a mirror that reflects, and sometimes distorts, these social constructs. Television shows, movies, news, and more recently, social media, profoundly shape our perceptions of gender and sexuality. They often reinforce stereotypes (like the notion that all men love sports or that women are more emotional than men), but they can also challenge and reshape these stereotypes.

Representation matters. Seeing diverse and realistic portrayals of people with different genders and sexual orientations can be affirming and empowering. It can also foster empathy and understanding in those who don't share those identities. For instance, a TV show that respectfully portrays a transgender character can help viewers understand and empathize with transgender people's experiences.

## Changing Norms and Acceptance Movements

Over time, society's views on gender and sexuality can and do change. Movements led by brave individuals and communities have challenged traditional norms and fought for rights and acceptance. The feminist movement, the gay rights movement, and the transgender rights movement are a few examples of how determined advocacy and activism can shift public opinion and policy.

These movements don't just aim to change laws; they also work to change hearts and minds. They promote the idea that all people, regardless of their gender or sexuality, deserve respect, rights, and opportunities. And while progress has been made, there is still much work to be done, especially in areas where discrimination and prejudice are deeply rooted.

In conclusion, the role of society and culture in shaping and reshaping gender and sexuality is immense. Through social constructs, media influence, and the tireless work of acceptance movements, we can see how dynamic and evolving our understanding of gender and sexuality can be. Recognizing this can help us become more open-minded and accepting, making our society more inclusive and just for everyone.

# Chapter 8: Health and Well-being

**Mental Health Issues in Gender and Sexual Minorities**

Gender and sexual minorities often face unique mental health challenges. This includes people who identify as lesbian, gay, bisexual, transgender, queer, or questioning (LGBTQ+). Due to societal stigma, discrimination, and sometimes even rejection from family and friends, individuals in these groups can experience higher levels of stress, anxiety, and depression.

It's important to understand that these mental health issues are not due to their gender identity or sexual orientation itself, but rather the way society treats these individuals. The feeling of being misunderstood, marginalized, or discriminated against can take a significant toll on one's mental health.

**Access to Healthcare and Support Systems**

Access to healthcare and supportive environments is crucial for the well-being of gender and sexual minorities. Unfortunately, many face barriers in accessing quality health care. These barriers can include lack of knowledgeable and sensitive healthcare providers, discrimination in healthcare settings, and sometimes even legal and policy obstacles.

Creating supportive environments, both in healthcare settings and in the community, is vital. This can be achieved through education and training of healthcare providers, anti-discrimination policies, and the establishment of support groups and community organizations.

**Strategies for Well-being and Resilience**

Despite these challenges, many gender and sexual minorities demonstrate incredible resilience. Resilience is the ability to cope with and overcome adversity. Here are some strategies that can help:

**Building a Supportive Network:** Surrounding oneself with understanding and supportive friends, family members, or groups can provide a sense of belonging and community.

**Self-acceptance:** Embracing one's own identity can be empowering. It's a journey that can involve exploring one's feelings and beliefs about themselves and learning to love and accept who they are.

**Seeking Professional Help:** Mental health professionals can provide a safe space to explore and cope with feelings, experiences, and challenges.

**Advocacy and Activism:** Getting involved in advocacy and activism can not only help in changing societal attitudes but also provide a sense of purpose and community.

**Self-Care Practices:** Engaging in activities that promote physical, emotional, and mental well-being, like exercise, meditation, or pursuing hobbies, can be very beneficial.

In conclusion, while gender and sexual minorities face specific challenges in terms of mental health and well-being, there are many paths to resilience and happiness. Access to supportive healthcare and communities, along with personal strategies for well-being, can greatly enhance the quality of life for these individuals. This chapter highlights the importance of understanding, acceptance, and support in fostering a healthier and more inclusive society.

# Chapter 9: The Future of Gender and Sexuality Psychology

**Emerging Trends and Future Research**

As we look to the future, the field of gender and sexuality psychology is poised to evolve in exciting ways. One of the key trends is the increasing recognition of the diversity of gender and sexual identities. Researchers are moving beyond binary concepts of male/female or gay/straight to explore a spectrum of identities, such as non-binary, pansexual, and asexual identities.

Another trend is the growing interest in how cultural, social, and environmental factors intersect with biology to shape gender and sexual identities. This holistic approach helps us understand these identities in a more nuanced and comprehensive way.

Future research will likely continue to explore these complex interactions. There's a growing interest in studying the experiences of underrepresented groups in gender and sexuality research, such as people of color, disabled individuals, and those from different socioeconomic backgrounds. This research is crucial for developing more inclusive theories and practices.

## The Role of Technology and Social Media

Technology and social media are playing an increasingly significant role in the field of gender and sexuality psychology. On one hand, they provide platforms for education, awareness, and community building. Online communities can offer vital support and information, especially for individuals who might feel isolated in their offline environments.

On the other hand, technology also presents challenges. Issues like online harassment and the spread of misinformation can negatively impact mental health and well-being. Navigating these challenges and harnessing the positive power of technology will be an important focus in the years ahead.

## Envisioning an Inclusive and Understanding Society

Looking forward, there's hope for a more inclusive and understanding society. This involves both celebrating diversity and actively working to reduce stigma and discrimination. Education plays a key role here, as does policy and advocacy work.

Inclusive policies in workplaces, schools, and healthcare systems can make a significant difference in the lives of gender and sexual minorities. Advocacy and activism will continue to be important in pushing for these changes.

We can also envision a society where mental health support is more accessible and tailored to meet the diverse needs of different gender and sexual identities. This would involve training more mental health professionals in understanding these issues and expanding access to supportive services.

In conclusion, the future of gender and sexuality psychology holds great promise. By embracing emerging trends, utilizing technology wisely, and working towards a more inclusive society, we can hope to better understand and support the diverse tapestry of human gender and sexuality. This chapter paints a picture of a future where differences are not just accepted but celebrated, and where everyone has the opportunity to live authentically and with dignity.

# Chapter 10: Conclusion: Embracing Complexity and Diversity

**Key Takeaways from the Book**

As we conclude our journey through the intriguing world of gender and sexuality psychology, let's reflect on the key takeaways:

**Gender and Sexuality are Spectrums:** We've learned that gender and sexuality are not binary but exist on broad spectrums, encompassing a wide range of identities and experiences.

**Influence of Society and Culture:** Our understanding of gender and sexuality is deeply influenced by societal norms and cultural contexts, which can change over time and differ across regions.

**Interplay of Biology and Environment:** While biology plays a role in gender and sexual development, environmental factors, personal experiences, and social influences are equally important.

**Intersectionality Matters:** The concept of intersectionality teaches us that gender and sexual identities intersect with other aspects of identity, such as race and class, creating unique experiences and challenges.

**Importance of Mental Health and Well-being:** Gender and sexual minorities often face specific challenges that can impact their mental health. Understanding, acceptance, and support are crucial for their well-being.

This book is more than just an exploration of concepts; it's a call to action. Here's how you can contribute to a more inclusive and understanding world:

**Educate Yourself and Others:** Continue learning about gender and sexuality. Share your knowledge with others to foster understanding and empathy.

**Challenge Stereotypes and Prejudices:** Be mindful of stereotypes and biases in your thinking and behavior. Challenge them in yourself and others.

**Support Inclusivity and Equality:** Advocate for policies and practices in your community and workplace that support inclusivity and equality for all genders and sexual orientations.

**Offer Support:** If you know someone struggling with their gender or sexual identity, offer your support. Sometimes, just being a good listener can make a big difference.

**Embrace Diversity:** Celebrate the diversity of human experience. Recognize that every individual's journey is unique and worthy of respect.

## The Path Forward in Understanding Gender and Sexuality

The path forward in understanding gender and sexuality is one of continuous learning and openness. As our society evolves, so too will our understanding of these aspects of human identity. By embracing complexity and diversity, we can create a world where everyone feels valued and included.

In this journey, remember that understanding gender and sexuality is not just an academic exercise; it's about understanding people, their experiences, and their perspectives. It's about building a world that recognizes and celebrates each person for who they are. This journey, filled with learning, empathy, and action, is one that we can all embark on together.

# About Freudian Trips

Welcome to Freudian Trips, your dedicated platform for diving deep into the world of psychology. We are more than just a YouTube channel or a book publisher. We are a beacon of enlightenment, making complex psychological concepts accessible and engaging for all.

Our YouTube channel is a rich repository of psychology made simple. We take the profound and often complex ideas from the world of psychology and break them down into digestible, easy-to-understand content. From the foundational theories of Freud to the cognitive insights of Piaget, we cover a broad spectrum of psychological schools and thoughts, making psychology accessible to everyone, regardless of their background or prior knowledge.

As a book publisher, we take the same approach, transforming intricate psychological theories into comprehensible narratives. Our books are not just collections of words, but vessels of wisdom that make psychology approachable and relatable. We believe that psychology should not be confined to academic circles, but should be available to all who seek to understand the human mind and behavior.

At Freudian Trips, we believe in the power of curiosity and the pursuit of knowledge. We are here to stoke the fires of your curiosity, to guide you on your intellectual journey, and to help you navigate the fascinating world of psychology.

If you are someone who is not afraid to question, to explore, and to learn, then you are in the right place. Join us on this journey of exploration, as we make psychology easy to understand, one concept at a time.

Be sure to visit our Youtube channel at: www.freudiantrips.com/youtube

You can also visit us on the web at www.freudiantrips.com

Welcome to The Freudian Trip community. Stay curious. Stay enlightened.